MIDLOTHIAN PUBLIC LIBRARY
3 1614 00170 5178

W9-BIU-801

Pebble Plus

BACKYARD ANIMALS

Chipmunks

by Mari Schuh

Consulting Editor: Gail Saunders-Smith, PhD

CAPSTONE PRESS
a capstone imprint

Pebble Plus is published by Capstone Press,
1710 Roe Crest Drive, North Mankato, Minnesota 56003
www.capstonepub.com

Library of Congress Cataloging-in-Publication Data
Schuh, Mari C., 1975– author.
Chipmunks / by Mari Schuh.
pages cm. — (Pebble plus. Backyard animals)
Summary: "An introduction to chipmunks, their characteristics, habitat, food, life cycle, and threats. Includes a hands-on activity related to wildlife watching" —Provided by publisher.
Audience: Ages 4–8.
Audience: K to grade 3.
Includes bibliographical references and index.
ISBN 978-1-4914-2085-0 (library binding) — ISBN 978-1-4914-2326-4 (ebook PDF)
1. Chipmunks—Juvenile literature. I. Title.
QL737.R68S3486 2015
599.36'4—dc23 2014032327

Editorial Credits
Nikki Bruno Clapper, editor; Juliette Peters, designer; Tracy Cummins, media researcher; Tori Abraham, production specialist

Photo Credits
Science Source: Tom McHugh, 17; Shutterstock: D and D Photo Sudbury, 11, Dale Wagler, 21, Daleen Loest, 9, Denis Dore, 15, Elena Elisseeva, Design Element, Cover Background, Julija Sapic, 5 Background, Manfred Schmidt, 7, Margaret M Stewart, 1, 13, 19, 22, Cover, N K, 17 Background, npine, 24, Pagina, Back Cover, PinkPueblo, Design Element, stock_shot, 5

Note to Parents and Teachers

The Backyard Animals set supports national curriculum standards for science related to life science and ecosystems. This book describes and illustrates chipmunks. The images support early readers in understanding the text. The repetition of words and phrases helps early readers learn new words. This book also introduces early readers to subject-specific vocabulary words, which are defined in the Glossary section. Early readers may need assistance to read some words and to use the Table of Contents, Glossary, Read More, Internet Sites, Critical Thinking Using the Common Core, and Index sections of the book.

Printed in the United States of America in Stevens Point, Wisconsin.
092014 008479WZS15

Table of Contents

Backyard Chipmunks

A small brown animal races across your picnic table. It stuffs a seed into its chubby cheeks. A chipmunk lives in your backyard!

Chipmunks are rodents
with sharp teeth and claws.
Their fur is brown with
black stripes. Their colors
help them hide in the woods.

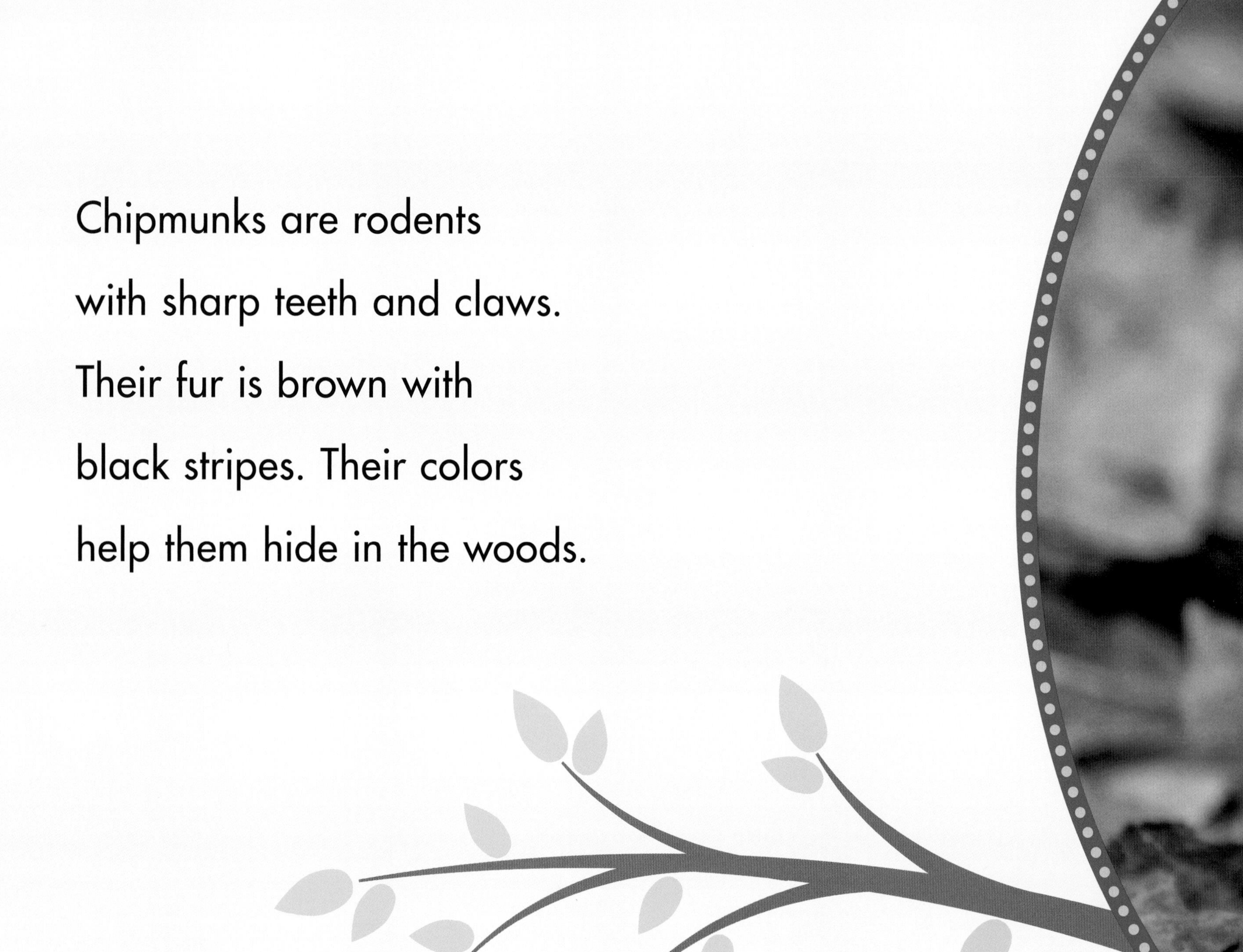

Chipmunks are the smallest animals in the squirrel family. They weigh about 5 ounces (140 grams).

Chipmunks have pouches in their cheeks. They stuff their pouches full of food. Then they take the food to their burrow.

Almost all chipmunks live
in North America.
Most of them dig burrows
under the ground. Some live
in trees, logs, or bushes.

What Chipmunks Do

Chipmunks store food for the winter. They gather nuts, seeds, and fruit. They also eat mushrooms, insects, and bird eggs.

Chipmunks mate in spring and summer. Females give birth to three to six pups. The pups are hairless and blind.

Soon the pups grow whiskers and fur. They stay with their mother for about two months. Chipmunks live for three to five years.

Wild Neighbors

Chipmunks are wild animals.
If you see a chipmunk,
do not feed it or go near it.
Instead, just enjoy watching
your wild neighbor.

Hands-On Activity: Tail Talk

How do chipmunks use their tails? Find out! Scientists wonder why chipmunks wag or fluff up their tails. Watch the chipmunks in your neighborhood. Take a notebook and a pencil with you. Each time you see a chipmunk move its tail or fluff it up, write down what is happening.

Is there another chipmunk nearby?

Does the chipmunk seem to be talking?

Does the chipmunk seem scared or angry?

Write down what you see.

Glossary

burrow—a hole or tunnel in the ground made or used by an animal

pouch—a part of a chipmunk's mouth that is like a pocket; chipmunks use their pouches to carry food to their burrow to store.

pup—a baby chipmunk

rodent—a mammal with long front teeth used for gnawing; chipmunks, squirrels, rats, and beavers are rodents.

Read More

Appleby, Alex. *I See a Chipmunk*. In My Backyard. New York: Gareth Stevens Pub., 2013.

Berger, Melvin and Gilda. *Chipmunks*. Discovering My World. New York: Scholastic, 2010.

Zobel, Derek. *Chipmunks*. Blastoff! Readers: Backyard Wildlife. Minneapolis: Bellwether Media, 2011.

Internet Sites

FactHound offers a safe, fun way to find Internet sites related to this book. All of the sites on FactHound have been researched by our staff.

Here's all you do:

Visit *www.facthound.com*

Type in this code: 9781491420850

Check out projects, games and lots more at
www.capstonekids.com

Critical Thinking Using the Common Core

1. How does a chipmunk use its pouch? (Key Ideas and Details)

2. Look at the pictures. Do you think it would be easy or difficult to spot a chipmunk? (Integration of Knowledge and Ideas)

Index

Word Count: 192
Grade: 1
Early-Intervention Level: 18